WITHDRAWN

FOR CREATING AND STICKING TO A BUDGET SUCCESSFULLY

DIANE BAILEY

ROSEN PUBLISHING

New York

Published in 2014 by The Rosen Publishing Group, Inc.
29 East 21st Street, New York, NY 10010

Library of Congress Cataloging-in-Publication Data

Bailey, Diane, 1966–.
Top ten secrets to creating and sticking to a budget successfully/ Diane Bailey.—1st ed.—New York: Rosen, © 2014
        p. cm.—(A student's guide to financial empowerment)
Includes bibliographical references and index.
ISBN: 978-1-4488-9360-7 (Library Binding)
ISBN: 978-1-4488-9369-0 (Paperback)
ISBN: 978-1-4488-9370-6 (6-pack)
1. Finance, personal—Juvenile literature.
2. Money—Juvenile literature. I. Title.
HG173.8 .B35 2014
332.024

Manufactured in the United States of America

CPSIA Compliance Information: Batch #S13YA: For further information, contact Rosen Publishing, New York, New York, at 1-800-237-9932.

Contents

For many teens, the best defense against an empty wallet is a thoughtful budget: a plan to manage money sensibly so that income stays in line with expenses.

Introduction

Stories in the news tell it all: a successful executive making $1 million a year suddenly finds himself broke. Meanwhile, a single mother manages to stay afloat on a job that barely pays minimum wage. How does that work?

In the phrase "money management," the key word is the second one. Some people, no matter how much money they earn, are always scrambling to make ends meet. Others live comfortably within their income, without seeming to make many sacrifices.

We all need money to live, but the old sayings are right: money doesn't buy happiness. It can buy some peace of mind, but even that's not guaranteed. Having more money doesn't necessarily make things easier. Often, people with high incomes believe they can afford much more than they really can.

Studies have shown that many teenagers don't have a good understanding of money. The credit card company Capital One conducted a poll on teenagers' financial habits and beliefs. It showed that almost half of teens did not know how to make or follow a budget. Just over 25 percent had discussed with their parents the difference between items that were "needs," versus those that were "wants."

Many teens don't have realistic knowledge of what things cost, or even what things are necessary to function in today's society. Most people have heard that the necessities of life are food, clothing, and shelter. While those are indeed the bare-bones requirements, it's also true that in order to get them, people depend on other items or services that cost money, such as transportation and insurance.

Good budgeting means being able to identify what your income and expenses are, deciding how to allocate your funds, and then making sure that how you spend money stays in line with your plan. A thoughtful budget takes into account not only how much you spend but also why you've chosen those particular goals.

Knowing how to budget and spend money isn't a difficult skill. It's simply one that takes a little knowledge and practice. Ultimately, financial success doesn't depend on how much money you earn—but how you use what you have.

Chapter 1

Understand the Purpose of a Budget

Budgeting is a necessary exercise in many households, but it also has a little bit of a bad name. Let's face it: budgeting is kind of boring. Who wants to draw up spreadsheets and spend hours with a calculator tallying up how much they spent on clothes and coffee? However, even if budgeting isn't your cup of tea (or iced coffee), it's still important to do it.

See Where It's Going

An old joke asks, "How do you make a small fortune?" The answer: "Well, first you start with a large one ..."

A good budget can help protect your fortune—even if it's small to begin with. Budgeting accomplishes several things. The most obvious one is that it clearly shows

Seemingly small purchases can often sink a budget. Smart budgeters will include funds to cover everyday treats such as coffee but will avoid indulging in too much of a good thing.

where, when, and how money is being spent. For someone who is struggling to make ends meet, or to save money for a larger purchase, a budget can prove invaluable because the numbers don't lie.

A dollar in a vending machine every day, or $2 on french fries from a fast-food restaurant, or $3 on a gourmet coffee … small things add up fast. It's simple math. Five bucks a day, every weekday, adds up to more than $100 a month on things that lasted less than an hour and could have easily been skipped.

Fascinating Financial Fact

A poll of fourteen- to eighteen-year-olds conducted by the Junior Achievement and the Allstate Foundation showed that in 2012 more than one-third of teens admitted that they did not budget or manage their money.

Identifying these trends is another function of a budget. They're specifically designed to track spending over time. Patterns of spending are what demonstrate a person's financial responsibility—or lack thereof. Also, by adding up the amount of money spent over the period of several months, it shows how easy it is to fritter away large sums, $1 at a time. Fortunately, the reverse is also true: $1 or $2 saved every day by eating lunch in instead of out, biking to work instead of driving, or deciding you don't really need another bottle of nail polish can also add up to a sizable amount after several weeks.

A budget helps reward "good behavior," financially speaking. Seeing the results of your spending habits written down in black and white reinforces when you've made good choices and when you've made poor ones. Knowing that your efforts to save helped you scrape together $50 for a concert ticket means you'll likely be able to do it again—and maybe for something bigger.

One Size Fits One

While there are definite guidelines for smart budgeting, there is no one-size-fits-all approach. Of course, many things will overlap from person to person. Many teenagers will spend money on food, clothing, transportation, and other discretionary expenses. However, each person's actual numbers will be different. More important, each person's priorities will be different.

Allocating money to keep her wardrobe up to date might be a "must" for one teen, but every person will have different priorities and must budget accordingly.

One person might choose to pay more for a cool leather jacket, while another prefers to shop secondhand in order to have extra funds for entertainment. Many teenagers have their own set of financial responsibilities that go beyond the fun stuff. They may have day-to-day expenses like gas and cell phones that their parents do not pay for, as well as longer-term goals like saving for college. A budget, therefore, should be a reflection of what you want right now and what you might want in the future.

Some people feel compelled to create a budget once they've landed in some financial trouble. In today's credit-heavy society, it's relatively easy to find yourself in debt—and sometimes that debt can be significant. However, while a budget is an absolute necessity if you're trying to pay down debt, it's not designed to be simply an "emergency measure." Instead, putting a budget in place before you're facing financial problems can help prevent having them.

Chapter 2

Set Goals

A budget isn't just a lot of columns of numbers. In fact, once you've decided to set a budget, the first thing you'll need isn't your calculator or some fancy financial software. Before you start to crunch the numbers, decide why you're budgeting and, more specifically, what you're budgeting *for*.

Small, Medium, or Large?

Setting goals is a critical step in budgeting. Goals should be specific and achievable. This does not mean they need to be instantaneously achievable. Many people choose to set goals in different stages. For money, a short-term goal might be having enough money to go to the movies on the weekend. A medium-term goal could be saving up for a new video game system. A long-term goal could be to buy a car or to have money to contribute to college expenses.

Planning can be especially tricky with long-term goals because they are so distant. Why bother to try and save for a car when there's no payoff for at least a year? A budget can help fight off the need for immediate gratification. Seeing how the money you put aside regularly adds up for the purchase of an end goal makes it more rewarding to stick to the program. It might be tempting to spend all your money now on clothes and entertainment. But at some point, you will be responsible for all of your expenses. Even if your parents have agreed to help you out for now, it's still important to learn the budgeting skills you'll need when they're no longer involved with your finances.

Driving can be fun and freeing, but buying a car will require some advance planning and saving. Also consider how to manage costs of gas, insurance, and maintenance.

Needs Versus Wants

Have you ever begged your parents for something, using the argument that you needed it? "You don't need it," they responded firmly. "You want it." That's not the answer most of us want to hear, but there's no denying that it's usually truthful. Most teenagers already have what they truly need—enough to eat, clothes to wear, and a roof over their heads.

In today's world, though, the line between "need" and "want" is a little fuzzy. Of course you won't drop dead on the sidewalk if you don't have a car, but there's an argument to be made that transportation is a need in today's society. Without it, you could not get to school or work. Health insurance is technically an extra, but the potential cost is enormous if someone were to get seriously ill or injured and didn't have insurance coverage.

Nonetheless, it's not always necessary to have a snazzy car or even a not-so-snazzy, car. For people living in rural areas, a car may be a real need. But a lot of people could get around by riding a bike or taking the bus. Many of the things we consider "needs" really aren't. Much of our money is spent on things that aren't strictly necessary.

Make It a Priority

After setting your financial goals, it's time to set your priorities. These two things aren't the same. A goal is an end. Prioritizing is the strategy you use to reach that goal. If your parents pay for some of the things you need

Tickets to a Rihanna concert will deliver a hit to most budgets. For many teens, this kind of pricey entertainment will require a sacrifice in some other area.

to live, you may have more flexibility in your budget. Adults living on their own usually have very little choice about whether they have to pay their rent (that'd be a yes) or buy their food. Teens, however, are often using money for

Fascinating Financial Fact

"Disposable" income is the amount of money left after subtracting taxes from income. Necessary expenses such as rent and food are paid from this amount. What's left for nonessential items or services is called "discretionary" income.

discretionary—nonessential—items. Concerts and clothes can be given up. A cell phone may seem like a necessity, and it's undeniably a very useful convenience. But it's not a necessity.

However, for the purposes of creating a budget, it's good to prioritize the most important things in your budget. Which would you rather do without—new clothes or a cell phone? If you feel you've got to have both, can you do without something else? The things that are most important to you are the things you budget for first.

1. My expenses are more than my income. Where are some good places to cut back?

2. I make more than enough money to cover my expenses, and I don't need to save up for anything big. Why should I bother with a budget?

3. Given my income and expenses, what percentage of my money should I allocate to savings?

4. What's a good approach to budgeting if I don't want to spend a lot of time on it?

5. How should I divide my money between everyday expenses and long-term savings goals?

6. Even with a budget, I spend too much. How can I change my behavior?

7. I spent too much in one of my budget categories, but had some leftover in another. Is there a way to make it balance out?

8. Should I try to get a credit card?

9. Is it better to put my money in a savings account or try the stock market for bigger returns?

10. I will have to go into debt to pay for college. How should I factor that into my budget?

Chapter 3

Take Stock of Your Spending

Budgets are real-world tools. No magic spell can transform them from a depressing list of negative numbers into a happily-ever-after fairy tale of finance.

That's the bad news.

The good news is, it's not that difficult to get a handle on spending. The first step to controlling it is to understand it.

Dear Diary

Diaries are places where people confess their deepest secrets. A budget diary isn't exactly for secrets, but it is a place that keeps you honest. Many people don't have a clear idea of how much they spend or what they're spending it on. By keeping a record, you can collect the basic information to make a budget.

Starting a budget from scratch isn't always the most effective approach. Sure, it's easy to say that you're going to spend a certain amount of money, but if you're like most people, you already have some established spending habits. It might just be a coffee in the morning or a few downloaded songs each week. But they're still there, and they still count. And—here's the kicker—if you're not even aware of those habits, they'll be very hard to break. Of course, you don't "accidentally" spend your money on a coffee—of course you know it costs something. However, it's easy to lose track of how much really goes toward small purchases.

Staying in touch is important, but in an era of cell phones and data plans, costs can add up. When making a budget, look for places where hidden expenses might be lurking.

Before you write your budget in earnest, make a record of all your financial transactions—both income and expenses. Write down everything you spend. Everything. Every penny.

It's best to do this over an extended period of time. A week might give you a snapshot of what you spend, but a month will be more accurate. Several months will be even more revealing.

Remember that many expenses are sporadic. If you pay for your cell phone, that expense comes regularly, every month (although the amount may vary depending on your plan). Other expenses, such as car insurance, may happen only once every few months. So, it's important not to forget about occasional bills like these.

As you do this, keep an eye out for things that you might cut back on. Also, try to get an idea of what your spending or saving "personality" is. Some people are naturally savers, while others want to spend money as soon as they get it.

Understanding Real Costs

Keeping a thorough record of your expenses helps you understand what things really cost, not just at the moment you pay for them, but over time as well. Another way to understand real-world costs is to participate in your family's budget. Most teens have heard their parents complain from time to time about all the bills they have to pay. However, many don't have a clear idea of what those bills really entail. It's easy to see that food and clothes cost money, and it's not so hard to figure out how much.

It's more difficult to figure out "soft" costs, like electricity or cable and Internet service, because teens often don't see

Fascinating Financial Fact

According to a 2011 report from the U.S. Department of Agriculture, a typical family will spend about $300,000 to raise a child until age eighteen (not including college). About 30 percent of the money will go to housing, 18 percent on education and child care, and 16 percent on food.

those bills. It's even harder to remember costs like insurance or taxes because those don't usually show up in a tangible way. If your parents are willing, ask them to share with you the bills they have to pay. This will help you get an understanding of how much things like taxes, insurance, and utilities cut into their paychecks.

A good way to practice budgeting is to take over a project within your family. For example, if your family is planning a vacation, offer to plan it within the budget your parents have set. This will help you learn how much things cost and how to balance priorities within a set limit.

Chapter 4

Pay Yourself First

A lot of things compete for your money. There are fixed expenses, such as car payments or a cell phone. Concert tickets and clothes come under the heading of variable costs. Some of these expenses are easier to control than others. You know that necessities have to come first, and you can skip a trip to the mall if you have to. But there's one category you shouldn't skip: yourself.

It's All About Me

Taking care of yourself doesn't mean springing for a nice dinner out. In fact, it doesn't mean spending at all. It means being aware of what you might need in the future and making sure you're ready. Any financial adviser will emphasize how important saving is to an overall financial plan. Having a nest egg gives you a cushion in case you face unforeseen expenses. Over time, this money can build into a sizable amount that can be put toward large costs such as college. Most teenagers aren't thinking about their retirement—after all, that's years in the future! However, saving money during your earning years means you won't have to worry when you are no longer working.

It's impossible to avoid the news of a struggling economy. Many teens have faced cutbacks in their own families. No one has escaped the larger budget cuts affecting school funding and other government programs. Compared to twenty years ago, jobs are more difficult to find, and they don't pay as much. Salaries are not keeping pace with rising prices.

The good news, for young people, is that even saving small amounts at a time—if you are consistent about it—can add

Walking the hallowed halls to a higher education doesn't come cheap: college is a huge expense for many teens and their parents and can challenge even the most well-planned budgets.

up. It's likely you won't miss a few dollars here and there, but if those same dollars are put into an interest-bearing savings account, or put to a longer-term investment, they will grow. In general, the longer the time period that a sum of money is committed to an investment, the higher the rate of return.

Too Much, Too Soon

Well, actually, no. "Too much, too soon" is a rule that doesn't apply when it comes to savings. It's that other rule, the one that says, "Too little, too late," that gets most people into trouble. Most teens have lots of years earning money ahead of them, but it's also true that young people can face enormous expenses early in their lives. The cost of college has skyrocketed in the last couple of decades, increasing at a rate that far outpaces any raise in salaries. Many teens simply can't afford to get an advanced education. If they do go to college, they may be saddled with thousands of dollars in student loans. Unfortunately, faced with these huge bills, some people simply give up. They feel that they will never be able to pull themselves out of debt. However, with college or other large expenses, a little pre-planning can go a long way.

Savings can also provide a safety net. If your car breaks down, for example, it will be a lot less disruptive if you have a little cash stashed away to put toward repairs.

How Much?

In general, it's a good idea to have a few categories for your savings. One can be for unforeseen costs, such as car

Fascinating Financial Fact

The "rule of 72" says that to calculate the number of years needed to double an amount of money, divide the interest rate into 72. For example, money invested at 4 percent will double in about eighteen years, assuming the interest is compounded annually. The rule works up to about a 20 percent interest rate.

repairs. Another can be devoted to a specific purpose, such as college, and used accordingly. A third category should be long-term, not to be touched except in an emergency.

When you're writing your budget, include contributions to each category. How much you put into each will vary depending on your priorities and commitments. Some experts advise that you put at least 10 percent of your income toward savings. Others are more aggressive, recommending that you try to cover your expenses with 60 percent of your income, and leave the remaining 40 percent to build a nest egg. One formula suggests that 30 percent go to spending, 30 to short-term savings, 30 to long-term savings, and 10 percent to charity.

What you ultimately decide, of course, is up to you. You may be in a place in your life where it's difficult to save much. On the other hand, you may be in a position where you have few true "needs" and can afford to save more. Here's one more rule for smart saving: if you can, do. You never know when you might need it.

Chapter 5

Put It in Writing

Even if math isn't your favorite (or best) subject in school, take heart. The arithmetic of budgeting isn't too hard, and you probably mastered the basics back in fourth grade. It's mostly addition and subtraction, with a little multiplication and division thrown in to keep things interesting.

Sort It Out

Pull out the spending diary you kept and take a look at it. Analyze your expenses and group them into categories. Some typical categories include clothes, entertainment, cell phone, and transportation. Do you eat out a lot? The cost of meals could fall under entertainment, or you could assign it to a separate category. If you take the bus to school or work, your bus fare will fall under transportation. If you ride your bike, it's reasonable to expect that maintenance would qualify as a transportation cost. If you have a car, then gas, maintenance, insurance, and car payments could all go into that category.

Decide how detailed you want your categories to be. You could choose to lump any expense with your car under transportation, or you might want to separate them. If you use computer software to keep track of your budget, the program can do both. It will show you the results in each specific category, as well as a general total under a broader heading.

Time It Right

One key decision in budgeting is to determine its time frame. In general, a budget works best when it corresponds to the times that you receive income or need to pay expenses. Younger teenagers, for example, may choose a weekly budget because that's when they get allowance. Older teenagers who are working may get a paycheck every two weeks. For them, a longer time frame will work better.

Don't forget sources of income or expenses that may be variable or irregular. For example, you may get $100 on your

Fascinating
Financial Fact

According to a 2012 study, teens spend almost 40 percent of their budget on fashion. About 7 percent goes to video games. Teen spending is increasing in many categories, including beauty products, restaurants, and electronic devices such as phones and tablet computers.

birthday, but of course, that happens only once a year. Work the amount into your budget by dividing the total amount by twelve. This is called prorating. Do the same with expenses, such as car insurance, that occur only a few times a year.

Choose a budgeting schedule that fits your daily life. A weekly budget may be too limiting. For example, you might stay home one weekend but then go to a big concert the next. If you budget $10 a week for entertainment, then you wouldn't have enough to splurge on your weekend out. However, a monthly budget would give you a bigger picture, showing that you can afford to have a big weekend of expenses as long as you are frugal on another. Many regular bills come only once a month. It's easy to overlook these in a weekly budget, but a monthly budget will take them into consideration.

Working with a longer-term budget is also helpful for learning the strategies of budgeting. With a weekly budget, if you blow all your money in the first day, you have to wait only six days before you're back in business. But with a monthly budget, you're forced to stretch your money if you want it to last. You'll have to make choices between competing "wants."

Whatever timetable you settle on, project it out for several months. This will provide a better idea of how much money is coming in and going out and help you plan for larger expenditures.

Do the Math

The whole key to budgeting is spending less than you earn. When you first write your budget, you will probably find that everything doesn't add up perfectly. You bring in $100 a month through allowance and babysitting, but you've identified $120

Most teens can work only part-time (if at all) and often at irregular jobs such as babysitting. Projecting income and planning for expenses is even more important in these circumstances.

worth of expenses. If this is the case, you'll need to trim back. You could chop out one whole expense—perhaps you decide a monthly subscription to an online movie site isn't worth it. Or, you might determine that all of your expenses are legitimate, but that you'll just have to cut back a little in each one.

In zero-based budgeting, everything must balance exactly. If you spend more in one category than you planned, it must come out of another. A rollover budget is slightly more flexible. With it, you can carry over the balance from one month—positive or negative—to the next. This type of budgeting lets you deal with larger expenses more easily.

Chapter 6

Get Organized

When your school notebooks are a wreck, it's difficult to find anything. You lose your homework and forget about assignments. If it gets really bad, your grades suffer. It's not that you don't know the material; it's that you're too disorganized to show that you know it. Budgeting can work the same way. You may decide that you're going to spend only a certain amount of money. But if you don't keep track of it, you can forget how much you've spent and easily go over.

Show Me the Money

Decide how you actually want to handle your cash—or *not* handle it. Some people use a simple "envelope" system. Label your envelopes with your categories, such as gas, dining out, and clothing purchases. At the beginning of each cycle, stock the envelopes with the amount of money you've budgeted for each category. Then, pay for your

Fascinating Financial Fact

Experts advise people to keep financial records such as bank statements and receipts for seven years. That's how long the Internal Revenue Service (IRS) has to audit a person's tax return.

expenses out of the corresponding envelope. Once you're out, you're out.

Using checks, debit cards, and even credit cards are other ways of paying. None of these involve using actual cash. Some people prefer this approach because it means less chance of losing their money or of having it stolen. The downside is that it's easier to overspend this way. When you don't see your money actually changing hands, you may forget that you've already spent the amount you had budgeted. However, if you can get into the habit of keeping track of all your transactions—including the ones you do by check or debit card—it's a good approach.

Of course, you'll still need to carry a little cash. If you decide to hit some garage sales on Saturday morning, you won't be able to use a credit card. But many

Budgeting doesn't have to be complicated. Divide and conquer financial foes with an envelope system that offers a simple way to categorize and manage expenses.

purchases can be made electronically, and millions of people pay their monthly bills that way. The world is increasingly becoming a cashless society, so it's a good idea to familiarize yourself with these processes.

Take It to the Bank

Even if you decide to handle most of your purchases using cash, it's still a good idea to have a bank account. As mentioned, when you reach adulthood, you will have to pay for many things electronically, so you'll need an account. In the meantime, a bank account gives you a way to protect and grow your money.

Basic savings accounts usually don't cost anything to open, and many do not require you to maintain a minimum balance. Even simple accounts like these, however, will pay you a small amount of interest. It's not much, but it's better than none. In the process you have your money in a safe place. If it's in a bank, it can't get stolen out of your wallet. Also, the federal government has laws to protect money held in banks. Even if the bank fails, you can get your money up to a certain amount.

It's also possible to link a savings account with a checking account. A checking account might not pay any interest, but it's a convenient way to get access to your money, and you can often move extra funds into your savings account.

Keeping Records

Keeping a budget means keeping records. Get in the habit of asking for a receipt whenever you buy something. If you're buying clothes, you'll want the receipt in case you need to return something. But don't stop there. You can't "return" your trip to the movies, but a paper trail will help you keep track of what you spend. If you work from your receipts, you might be surprised at the things you have forgotten about. Even after you've used the receipts to manage your budget, don't throw them away. Keep a couple of boxes: one for receipts that you've been through and are recorded in your budget and another for ones that you'll do in the next batch. Occasionally you might find a problem or mistake, and need to refer back to your original records (the receipts).

It's easy just to toss receipts into the trash, but they can prove valuable when it comes time to figure out where your money went and how to plan for the future.

Also, decide whether you want to keep your budget electronically or with a pencil and paper. Either one will work. For simple budgets, you can use a notebook with a few columns: income, expenses, and overall balance. More complicated budgets will benefit from using a spreadsheet on a computer, with a way to automatically do calculations. Special budgeting software programs will include additional functions, such as categorizing expenses.

Chapter 7

Work the System

You know what you earn, and what you spend. You've got goals and a plan to get there. You've written a budget that gives you a manageable approach to saving and spending. Now comes the hard part: sticking to it.

Showing Discipline

Probably the most challenging part of budgeting isn't the planning, but the doing. It's tough when you want to go out with your friends, or indulge in a snack, but your budget tells you no. If you don't actually have the money in your pocket, then it's easier—you have no choice. But the point of budgeting is not to run out of money and force yourself into doing without. It's consciously deciding to say no, even when you have the power to say yes. It takes discipline to learn to make choices like that. And it takes practice. Fortunately, once you start to see the results of saving money, it gets easier.

People who are trying to diet or exercise often team up with someone else for help. This can work for budgeting, too. If you think you need a little help to stay on track, enlist a friend to be your "budget buddy." Your budgets don't have to look alike, of course, because you will probably have different priorities. But you can help each other look for weaknesses in your strategies. More important, you can help each other with your resolve. Your parents may also be able to help. They'll likely want you to succeed, so ask for their advice on how to keep your spending under control.

Credit cards, debit cards, and ATMs make it easy—often *too* easy—to spend money. Fight back by getting friends to help you stay on track, and be sure to return the favor!

One trick to successful budgeting is to limit your trips to the ATM. Twenty dollars here and there adds up fast. If you withdraw cash, do it once a week, and make the money last until your next trip. Resist the urge to go back.

Find Incentives

Remember that list of goals you made? You should. It's not supposed to be the kind of thing that you write up, stick in a drawer (or a computer file), and forget about. Knowing that you are actively working toward something is a great incentive. When you say no to one thing, remind yourself that you're also saying yes to something else. Budgeting is not just about giving things up—it's about getting other things later on. You can't get everything you want, so the trick is deciding what you want more.

Look for some creative ways to manage your budget. For example, your parents likely support the idea of you saving money. If you're doing that, you might be able to get them to help you. Perhaps they would consider matching some of the funds you're putting away for college.

It's also okay to splurge occasionally. The key word here is—you guessed it—occasionally. If you spring for lunch at the local deli every day, it no longer qualifies as a splurge. It's now a regular expense for which you must budget accordingly. But, if you know you can give yourself a little reward now and then, it makes it easier to stick to your overall budget.

Even though the key to budgeting isn't about making more money, it's also true that if you really want something,

Finding employment can be especially tough for teens with little or no work experience, but sometimes pounding the pavement can land you a job and ease budget constraints.

you may be motivated to find more sources of income. If you're saving up for something big, or find yourself strapped for cash on a daily basis, consider finding a part-time job

Fascinating Financial Fact

Banks charge customers hefty fees for using ATMs that are not from their own banks. The average cost is about $3.80 per transaction, according to a 2011 study.

or doing odd jobs around the house or for your neighbors. Sometimes, it's easier to increase your income than to try to scrimp any more. If this is a viable option, then take advantage of it.

Finally, remember that a budget is a tool, not a rule. Build in some flexibility. If you really want to overspend in one category, allow a little wiggle room where you can make it up by cutting back in another. Save up extra funds in a slow month so you can use them, guilt-free, if there's a big month of entertainment coming up later in the year.

MYTHS
AND
FACTS

Myth

A budget is necessary only for getting out of debt or if you don't have very much money.

FACT

A budget can help keep you from going into debt in the first place, which can save money in the long run. It also helps you put aside money for emergencies.

Myth

Budgeting means you have to be good at math.

FACT

Only if you're going to manage the accounts at a multinational firm. For a personal budget, all you need are basic math skills—or a calculator.

Myth

If I budget my money, I won't have anything to spend on fun stuff.

FACT

The point of a budget isn't to suck the fun out of everything. Instead, it's designed to help you keep track of your money—and some of that can be spent on fun.

Chapter 8

Think Thrifty

Even people who earn a lot of money can run into trouble if they're not careful about their spending habits. Fortunately, there are many ways to cut your spending just by doing some thrifty thinking—and many of them can be fun.

Savvy Shopping

You've probably seen them at the store: those wallet warriors with fists full of coupons and sale items. It's relatively painless to save money just by being a shrewd shopper. Waiting for sales is one obvious solution. You'll probably be able to get by just fine for another week or two without another pair of jeans. Nonessential consumer items are prime targets to go on sale when stores need to move their stock.

Many major department stores offer regular coupons online or in the newspaper. Some of them have a minimum dollar limit. For example, if you spend $50 or more, you get 15 percent off

Save paper if you can, but not if there's a coupon printed on it. Smart shoppers know to let stores save money for them by using coupons and shopping for bargains.

the total bill. Even if you don't have $50 worth of merchandise—and that's great for your budget!—you can team up with a friend and combine your purchases so that you can take advantage of the discount. Coupons can have a downside, however. Resist the urge to go shopping just for the sake of using a coupon. If you wouldn't have bought something without a coupon, don't buy it with one. Avoid buying something on the spur of the moment—impulse buying. Instead, wait a set period of time before you buy anything. Ask yourself if you still really want the item after a day or a week has passed.

Fascinating Financial Fact

According to a report by NCH Marketing Services, shoppers used $4.6 billion in coupons in 2011. That marked a 12.2 percent increase over 2010, indicating that the recession was inspiring people to look for cost-cutting measures.

Also, look for items secondhand. Not everything has to be brand-new to be useful. Sometimes, you don't have to buy at all. Borrow something you'll need only once or twice, or trade items you don't want for those that you do. You might also be able to share a big purchase. If you and your sister both want a game system, maybe you can split the cost.

Sweat the Small Stuff

One of the most painless ways to save money is simply to eliminate a handful of small things, such as a soda or magazine. That's not to say that you can't indulge in some of these small pleasures—after all, part of the fun of having some spending money is to treat yourself occasionally. But they're not things you can't live without, and they certainly don't have to be things that you get every day.

Many buying habits really aren't about the purchase at all. They're part of an overall pattern of behavior. You may have gotten in the habit of stopping by a convenience store every day after school and buying a candy bar while you're there. By removing the destination, you can often get rid of the purchasing pattern as well. If you feel like you really can't go without your after-school sugar fix, then try another approach: buy a whole pack of candy bars in bulk, for less money, and have one when you get home.

One trick to saving is to collect your loose change. You probably won't miss that seventeen cents you get in change after buying a soda, but don't let it fall out of your pocket into the couch cushions. Instead, put it in a jar. After a few months, take it to the bank and convert it into some real cash.

A penny saved is a penny earned. Every little bit helps. Those sayings may sound silly and old-fashioned, but there's a reason people recite them: they're true.

Free Fun . . . or At Least Reduced-Price

The best things in life . . .

You can finish that sentence, right? Most people have heard that the things in life that really count are free. Many of the times you spend money are probably when you are spending time with your friends. But socializing doesn't require much funding—and sometimes none at all.

Try pooling your money for some snacks and the rental price of a DVD, instead of paying the full freight at the movie theater. Play basketball in the park instead of going to the bowling alley. Even better, make a deal with your friends to team up to do some volunteer work. You'll still get to spend time together, you'll save money, and you'll be doing a good deed—all at the same time!

Chapter 9

Paper or Plastic?

Cash is one way to pay for things. There's so-called "hard cash," which is paper money and coins. However, paying by check or using a debit card are also ways of paying cash. A check simply allows the holder to have your bank distribute the amount of money you designated on the check. Even though you're not handing over dollar bills, however, the money is already in your account. It is part of your cash holdings. Debit cards work essentially the same way. Instead of using a paper check, however, the transaction is done electronically. Again, though, the withdrawal comes from funds you already have—your cash. Prepaid credit cards are actually not credit cards at all; they are just often issued by credit card companies. However, the card is paid for in advance and then functions as a debit card.

How Credit Works

Credit works very differently. By definition, when you purchase something with credit, you are borrowing money and promising to repay it at a later

Credit cards are compact and convenient, but be careful not to get too comfortable. It's easy to get carried away, and they can turn your finances into a blur.

date. Although there is a convenience to credit, it comes with a price. Usually, unless you repay the money within a short time frame, you have to pay interest on the money you borrow.

The most well-known form of credit purchasing is a credit card. Credit card agreements come with certain terms. For example, the holder will have a credit limit. This can vary. People who have a limited credit history, or people who have had problems with credit, may have a low limit, perhaps a few hundred dollars. People who have established credit and have demonstrated the ability to meet the terms of repaying money can often get higher limits.

Most credit cards allow the borrower a certain amount of time to borrow the money for "free." Each month, the credit card company bills you for your purchases. If you pay off the entire balance before the due date (usually two or three weeks later), you do not have to pay interest. If you do not pay it all, the unpaid balance begins racking up interest.

Fascinating Financial Fact

Credit cards were first used in the United States in the 1920s. Individual companies such as hotels would provide them to regular customers. Later, bank-issued cards let customers buy from many different merchants. The bank acted as a middleman, paying the merchant and collecting from the customer.

Advantages and Disadvantages

Credit card interest rates typically run much higher than those of other forms of borrowing. Credit companies may charge 16 or 17 percent interest, or more, on the unpaid balance. It can be easy to get into deep debt using credit cards, and it's difficult to get out. Besides the high interest rates, credit card companies also charge fines if you do not pay at least a minimum amount each month. In addition, the interest continues to accrue each month on both the unpaid balance and any new purchases.

There are, however, some advantages to using credit cards. For one thing, they are a convenient way to pay. You do not need to carry cash to make purchases (although this can also be solved by using a debit card). Many credit cards also offer a cash back program. For each $1 spent, the holder is paid a small amount back, about a penny. If you were going to spend that money anyway, it's a relatively easy way to rake in a few extra bucks. Finally, there is a grace period of a few weeks during which the buyer does not have to pay interest on any purchases. The money needed to pay can then stay in an interest-bearing account for a little longer.

Using a credit card can also help you build a credit history. At some point, you may need to borrow money for large expenses, such as education or to buy a car. Lenders are more likely to approve your loan if you can show that you are responsible about your credit. A good credit history can also help you get a lower interest rate.

It's vital to use credit cards responsibly. Unless you plan to pay off your balance, in full, every month, it's better to avoid using them. One idea is to obtain a card that you use only in case of emergencies. Don't put it in your wallet, where you'll be tempted to use it when you're out shopping. Instead, leave it at home. It will be available if you need it, but not *too* available!

Chapter 10

Revisit and Revise

Most skills take some time to learn and then more time to master. In that way, budgeting isn't unlike learning a musical instrument or playing a sport. It's probably unrealistic to expect your first attempt at writing a budget to work out perfectly. It might not even work at all. But with a little practice, you can learn how to identify your goals, adjust your spending behavior, and create a budget that works for you.

Making Mistakes

From time to time, almost everyone makes some kind of financial misstep. They buy something that costs too much. They wait too long to pay a bill. They don't save enough for a large purchase. If this happens, don't assume that you simply have no flair for finance and then give up. Instead, look back to see how the

Fascinating Financial Fact

Minors (people under eighteen) can have IRAs (individual retirement accounts), as long as the account is held by an adult who acts as a guardian, although the minor is the owner for tax purposes. The maximum contribution is $5,000 or 100 percent of earned income, whichever is less.

mistake happened. Did you forget to keep good records? Did you know you couldn't afford something, but buy it anyway, figuring you'd "work it out later"? Did you neglect to take a long-term view so that you had an accurate picture of what expenses you'd be facing? Whatever the cause, take the steps to fix it so you don't fall into the same trap again.

In addition, take responsibility for the mess you've made. Hopefully, it isn't too big of a mess. One advantage to learning budgeting as a teen is that you're typically dealing with much smaller amounts of money than you will be as an adult living on your own. If at all possible, avoid asking your parents to bail you out. If you absolutely must borrow money, do it on real-world terms: establish an interest rate that you will pay on the borrowed money and the time frame in which you must pay it back. (Be sure to include your payments when you redo your budget!)

Investing

As you become more comfortable and experienced with the processes of budgeting, spending, and saving, you can move on to more advanced forms of money management. Hopefully, you've learned a little about saving and earning interest by having a bank account. While these can pay you a small amount of interest, other types of investments can deliver much more. A certificate of deposit (CD) will typically pay better interest than a savings account because you agree to leave the money alone for a certain period of time. This might be only a few months or it could be several years. Other forms of investments are retirement accounts, mutual funds, and individual stocks. Many books cover how different investments work and offer guidance on becoming a smart investor.

Moving Forward

Each person needs a personal budget that reflects his or her own individual needs and preferences. Even then, however, one budget won't last forever. It might last a year, or it might last only a week! It's important to go back and review your budget regularly. You may have underestimated how much you can save, or you might find that one of your regular expenses is higher than you anticipated. Instead of saving up for concert tickets, you might decide to put your savings toward a car. It's okay for your goals to change. Try not to be too fickle, however. If you are saving for college, don't change your mind just because that new game system looks so appealing.

Paperwork isn't always fun, but keeping a close eye on your finances will let you see the big picture and ensure that potential problems don't get out of control.

Finally, make budgeting a habit. Set aside a little time each week—say, half an hour—to put your finances in order. Are you meeting your goals? If there are problems, tinker with the numbers to look for different solutions. A budget problem won't go away if you ignore it, but if you catch it early, it doesn't have to turn into a huge headache.

Money is essential for anyone. Using it wisely can bring you financial independence and freedom and give you choices about what you can do. As a teenager, you have one huge thing in your favor: time. Learning to budget and manage your money now will give you even more options in the future.

Glossary

accrue To add up, or accumulate.

allocate To assign to a category.

audit To perform a review, or check for accuracy.

cashless Using only electronic methods of payment but no "hard cash."

compound interest Interest that is earned and then added into the original principal.

correspond To match or agree.

discretionary Something that is by choice.

expenditure An expense, or outflow of money.

fickle Easily influenced, often by unimportant factors.

frugal Not wasteful; careful and economical about spending money.

guardian Someone who is legally in charge of overseeing the affairs of someone else.

interest Extra money charged on a loan.

minimum wage The lowest amount of money someone can be paid per hour, as determined by state or federal law.

outpace To proceed at a faster rate than something else.

prorate To divide the cost of something over a period of time or among several categories, according to its use.

rate of return The percentage of money gained or lost on an investment.

rollover budget A budget that allows amounts (both positive or negative) to be carried over from one month to the next and incorporated into the new budget.

sporadic Irregular, or not according to a schedule.

spreadsheet A type of document that organizes information by using rows and columns to create individual data cells.

tangible Real or actual; something that can be noticed or documented.

viable Practical; achievable.

zero-based budgeting A form of budgeting that requires everything to be accounted for, so that the balance is neither positive nor negative.

For More Information

Canadian Foundation for Economic Education (CFEE)
110 Eglinton Avenue West, Suite 201
Toronto, ON M4R 1A3
Canada
(416) 968-2236
Web site: http://www.cfee.org
The CFEE is a nonprofit organization that works to promote
the economic capabilities and skills of Canadians by
working in areas such as research, curriculum develop-
ment, and strategic planning.

Council for Economic Education
122 East 42nd Street, Suite 2600
New York, NY 10168
(212) 730-7007 or (800) 338-1192
Web site: http://www.councilforeconed.org
The Council for Economic Education works to provide
economic and financial education to schools in the
United States and around the world.

The Financial Planning Association
7535 E. Hampden Avenue, Suite 600
Denver, CO 80231
(800) 322-4237

Web site: http://www.fpanet.org

The Financial Planning Association is a membership organization of financial planning experts that connects consumers with qualified professionals.

Money Management International

14141 Southwest Freeway, Suite 1000

Sugar Land, TX 77478

(866) 889-9347

Web site: http://www.moneymanagement.org

Money Management International is a credit counseling agency that provides financial guidance, help with debt management, bankruptcy counseling, and educational programs to individuals.

The National Association of Personal Finance Advisors

3250 North Arlington Heights Road, Suite 109

Arlington Heights, IL 60004

(847) 483-5400

Web site: http://www.napfa.org

The National Association of Personal Financial Advisors is a membership organization of financial advisors connecting consumers with these professionals.

National Endowment for Financial Education (NEFE)

1331 17th Street, Suite 1200

Denver, CO 80202

(303) 741-6333

Web site: http://www.nefe.org

The NEFE sponsors educational programs, offers consumer resources, and engages in research to help
further financial education and responsibility.

Web Sites

Due to the changing nature of Internet links, Rosen Publishing
has developed an online list of Web sites related to the subject of this book. This site is updated regularly. Please use
this link to access the list:

http://www.rosenlinks.com/SGFE/Bdgt

For Further Reading

Bamford, Janet. *Street Wise: A Guide for Teen Investors.* Hoboken, NJ: Bloomberg Press, 2011.

Bellenir, Karen, ed. *Cash and Credit Information for Teens: Tips for a Successful Financial Life.* Detroit, MI: Omnigraphics, 2009.

Bellenir, Karen, ed. *Debt Information for Teens: Tips for a Successful Financial Life.* Detroit, MI: Omnigraphics, 2011.

Bielagus, Peter. *Quick Cash for Teens: Be Your Own Boss and Make Big Bucks.* New York, NY: Sterling Publishing, 2009.

Butler, Tamsen. *The Complete Guide to Personal Finance: For Teenagers and College Students.* Ocala, FL: Atlantic Publishing Group, 2010.

Cassedy, Patrice. *Finance: Careers for the Twenty-First Century.* Farmington Hills, MI: Lucent, 2009.

Chatzky, Jean. *Not Your Parents' Money Book: Making, Saving, and Spending Your Own Money.* New York, NY: Simon & Schuster Books for Young Readers, 2010.

Donovan, Sandy. *Budgeting Smarts: How to Set Goals, Save Money, Spend Wisely, and More.* Minneapolis, MN: Lerner Publishing, 2012.

Ferguson Publishing. *Ferguson's Careers in Focus: Financial Services.* New York, NY: Ferguson Publishing, 2011.

Fischer, James. *The Power to Do Good: Money and Charity.* Broomall, PA: Mason Crest Publishers, 2010.

Furgang, Kathy. *How the Stock Market Works*. New York, NY: Rosen Publishing, 2010.

Gerber, Larry. *Top 10 Tips for Developing Money Management Skills*. New York, NY: Rosen Publishing, 2012.

Hansen, Mark, and Kevin Ferber. *Success 101 for Teens: Dollars and Sense for a Winning Financial Life*. St. Paul, MN: Paragon House, 2012.

Hollander, Barbara Gottfried. *Paying for College: Practical, Creative Strategies*. New York, NY: Rosen Publishing, 2010.

Magill, Elizabeth, ed. *College Financing Information for Teens: Tips for a Successful Financial Life*. Detroit, MI: Omnigraphics, 2011.

Peterson's Publishing. *Don't Break the Bank: A Student's Guide to Managing Money*. Lawrenceville, NJ: Peterson's, 2012.

Saddleback Publishing. *The 21st Century Lifeskills Handbook: Managing Money*. Costa Mesa, CA: Saddleback Publishing, 2012.

Simons, Rae. *A Guide to Teaching Young Adults About Money*. Broomall, PA: Mason Crest Publishers, 2010.

Thompson, Helen. *Cost of Living*. Broomall, PA: Mason Crest Publishers, 2010.

Thompson, Helen. *Investing Money*. Broomall, PA: Mason Crest Publishers, 2010.

Vickers, Rebecca. *101 Ways to Be Smart About Money*. Chicago, IL: Heinemann-Raintree, 2011.

Women's Foundation of California. *It's a Money Thing: A Girl's Guide to Managing Money*. San Francisco, CA: Chronicle Books, 2008.

Bibliography

Agora Financial For Families. "Getting Your Kids Involved in Developing a Budget." Retrieved May 12, 2012 (http://mason.gmu.edu/~tguingab/agora/Money /Money02B-03.html).

BankofAmerica.com. "Money Management for Teenagers." Retrieved May 12, 2012 (http://learn.bankofamerica .com/articles/money-management/money-management -for-teenagers.html).

CreditScore.net. "Financial Education for Teens." Retrieved May 26, 2012 (http://www.creditscore.net/financial -education-for-teens).

Dance, Robin. "Allowances: Teaching Teens How to Manage Their Money." SimpleMom.net, March 2, 2011. Retrieved May 24, 2012 (http://money.msn.com/family-money /8-crucial-money-lessons-for-teens-freedman.aspx).

Freedman, Donna. "8 Crucial Money Lessons for Teens." MSN Money, March 27, 2012. Retrieved May 24, 2012 (http://money.msn.com/family-money/8-crucial-money -lessons-for-teens-freedman.aspx).

Lawrence, Judy. *The Budget Kit: The Common Cents Money Management Workbook.* Chicago, IL: Dearborn Trade Publishing, 2004.

Money-Management-Works.com. "Teenagers Money Management." Retrieved May 26, 2012 (http://www

.money-management-works.com/teenagers-money-management.html).

MoneyandStuff.info. "Savvy Stuff: Top 10 Budgeting Basics for Teens." Retrieved May 24, 2012 (http://www.moneyandstuff.info/budgetingbasics.html).

Ramsey, Dave. *The Money Answer Book*. Nashville, TN: Thomas Nelson, 2010.

Rice, Danielle. "Do Teens Know the Basics of Personal Finance?" *Piedmont Family Magazine*. Retrieved May 26, 2012 (http://caopublications.org/FinSection.asp?File=TeenFinancialLiteracy.html).

Sander, Jennifer Basye, and Peter Sander. *The Pocket Idiot's Guide to Living on a Budget*. New York, NY: Alpha Books, 2005.

Shelly, Susan. *The Complete Idiot's Guide to Money for Teens*. New York, NY: Alpha Books, 2001.

Skyhorse Publishing. *10,001 Ways to Live Large on a Small Budget*. New York, NY: Skyhorse Publishing, 2009.

Thakor, Manisha, and Sharon Kedar. *On My Own Two Feet*. Avon, MA: Adams Media, 2007.

Tucci, Paul. *The Handy Personal Finance Answer Book*. Canton, MI: Visible Ink Press, 2012.

Velshi, Ali, and Christine Romans. *How to Speak Money: The Language and Knowledge You Need Now*. Hoboken, NJ: Wiley Publishing, 2012.

Wiley Publishing. *Managing Your Money All-in-One for Dummies*. Hoboken, NJ: Wiley Publishing, 2009.

Index

About the Author

Diane Bailey has written about twenty-five nonfiction books for teens, on subjects ranging from sports to states to celebrities. Her first novel, *Murder a Cappella*, a murder mystery, was published in 2012. Diane also works as an editor for other children's authors. She has two sons and two dogs and lives in Kansas.

Photo Credits

Cover Klaus Mellenthin/Getty Images; p. 4 SelectStock/ the Agency Collection/Getty Images; p. 8 Chris Hondros/ Getty Images; p. 10 Robert Nickelsberg/Getty Images; p. 13 Monkey Business/Thinkstock; pp. 14-15 Noel Vasquez/ Getty Images; pp. 19, 29, back cover, multiple interior pages background image iStockphoto/Thinkstock; p. 23 Kevork Djansezian/Getty Images; p. 31 Hemera/Thinkstock; p. 33 Jack Hollingsworth/Photodisc/Thinkstock; p. 35 Purestock/ Thinkstock; pp. 36–37 © AP Images; p. 41 Stan Honda/ AFP/Getty Images; p. 43 Jessica Boone/Photodisc/Getty Images; p. 46 Peter Cade/Iconica/Getty Images; p. 52 JGI/ Jamie Grill/Blend Images/Getty Images.

Designer: Michael Moy; Editor: Bethany Bryan;
Photo Researcher: Amy Feinberg